M
16.95 MCR

WIT EVANSTON PUBLIC LIBRARY

S0-DXO-660

3 1192 01209 0369

x962 Parke.L

Parker, Lewis K.

Egypt /

MAY 3 0 2003

Discovering Cultures

Egypt

Lewis K. Parker

EVANSTON PUBLIC LIBRARY
CHILDREN'S DEPARTMENT
1703 ORRINGTON AVENUE
EVANSTON, ILLINOIS 60201

BENCHMARK BOOKS

MARSHALL CAVENDISH
NEW YORK

This book is dedicated to all my family members, especially my grandchildren—L.K.P.

With thanks to Jennifer Houser Wegner, Ph.D., University of Pennsylvania Museum of Archaeology and Anthropology, for the careful review of this manuscript.

Benchmark Books
Marshall Cavendish
99 White Plains Road
Tarrytown, New York 10591-9001
www.marshallcavendish.com

Text copyright © 2003 by Marshall Cavendish Corporation
Map and illustrations copyright © 2003 by Marshall Cavendish Corporation

All rights reserved. No part of this book may be reproduced or utilized in any form or by any means electronic or mechanical, including photocopying, recording, or by any information storage and retrieval system, without written permission from the copyright holders.

All Internet sites were available and accurate when sent to press.

Library of Congress Cataloging-in-Publication Data

Parker, Lewis K.
Egypt / by Lewis K. Parker.
p. cm. — (Discovering cultures)
Summary: Highlights the geography, people, food, schools, recreation, celebrations, and language of Egypt.
Includes bibliographical references and index.
ISBN 0-7614-1519-X
1. Egypt—Juvenile literature. [1. Egypt.] I. Title. II. Series.
DT49 .P375 2003
962—dc21   2002015305

Photo Research by Candlepants Incorporated

Front Cover Photo: Roger Wood/Corbis

The photographs in this book are used by permission and through the courtesy of; *Richard T. Nowitz*: 1, 28 (right), 36, 40. *Getty Images*: 4-5; Stone/John Lawrence, 14; Stone/Will & Deni McIntyre, 15, back cover; Allsport/Shaun Botterill, 30; The Image Bank/Jeff Rotman, 32-33. *Corbis*: Farrell Grehan, 6; Premium Stock, 8-9; Ron Watts, 10; Dallas & John Heaton, 11; Adam Woolfit, 16-17; Historical Picture Archive, 18; Richard T. Nowitz, 19; Owen Franklin, 20-21; SABA/Thomas Hartwell, 22, 26, 27; Peter M. Wilson, 23; Sandro Vannini, 34; Gary Trotter/Eye Ubiquitous, 37; Jeffery L. Rotman, 38; AFP/Mohammed Al-Sehiti, 41; Kevin Fleming, 44 (top); Archivo Iconographico, 45. *Malie Rich-Griffith/Infocusphotos.com*: 12. *Steven Needham/Envision*: 24. *Christine Osborne Pictures*: 28 (left), 39. *AP Photo/Enric Marti*; 31. *Squashpics.com/Steve Line*: 44 (left).

Map and illustrations by Salvatore Murdocca
Book design by Virginia Pope

Cover: *The Great Sphinx guards the pyramids of Giza;* Title page: *Egyptian girl in traditional dress*

Printed in Hong Kong
1 3 5 6 4 2

Turn the Pages...

Ezayak!

That is what you would hear if you traveled to Egypt. It is an Arabic word that means "How are you?" It is a greeting to a friend.

Many visitors come to Egypt to see the ancient pyramids and to ride camels. But Egypt is more than that. Let's take a look...

A boy welcomes visitors to Egypt.

Where in the World Is Egypt?

Egypt is located on two continents. Most of Egypt is located on the northeast corner of Africa, but part of the country is also on the southwest tip of Asia. Egypt is a medium-sized country. Its size almost equals the states of Texas, Oklahoma, and Arkansas combined. Libya is Egypt's neighbor on the west. Sudan borders the

The Nile River flows through Egypt.

Mediterranean Sea

Alexandria

• Suez Canal

★ Cairo

Sinai Peninsula

• Jabal Katrinah

Gulf of Suez

Arabian Desert

Nile River

Red Sea

N
NW   NE
W   E
SW   SE
S

south and Israel lies to the northeast. Egypt's northern coastline is the Mediterranean Sea. The Red Sea is to its east.

From space, Egypt appears to be mostly desert. The Nile River winds like a ribbon through the desert. The Nile is the longest river in the world. It flows 4,145 miles (6,671 kilometers). The Nile starts in the mountains in countries south of Egypt and flows north into the Mediterranean Sea. There it divides into dozens of smaller rivers. This area is called the Nile Delta.

Because Egypt is mainly desert, only about 5 percent of the land can be used for farming. Most farming takes place in the green valley created by the Nile River. The main crops are cotton, sugarcane, dates, olives, wheat, and rice. Egyptians pump water from the Nile to irrigate, or water, their crops.

The Nile Valley is also where most Egyptians live. Cairo, the capital, is located in the Nile Valley. Cairo is a crowded city with more than 15 million people.

Cairo at night

It is also a city where modern skyscrapers are built close to mud and brick houses. Alexandria, Egypt's second largest city, is on the Mediterranean. It is the country's main seaport.

The Western Desert covers most of Egypt. This empty desert is known for its sand dunes that drift like waves. On a very hot day, the temperature may reach 125 degrees.

It is not surprising that only a few people live in the Western Desert. They live near oases that dot the sand. An oasis is where water comes up from underground and forms ponds and wells.

The Eastern Desert is also called the Arabian Desert. It slopes eastward to the hills along the coast of the Red Sea. Not many people live in this desert either, but there are a few small towns.

Farther east is the Sinai Peninsula. The Gulf of Suez and the Suez Canal separate this peninsula from the rest of the country. Red and brown deserts and

Sand dunes in the Western Desert

mountains cover the Sinai. Swamps and palm trees appear at the northern edge of the peninsula. Many people come here to enjoy the white sandy beaches at the shore. Gebel Katherina (Mount Catherine) is also in the Sinai. It is Egypt's highest mountain.

Egypt's climate is hot and dry. The country has two seasons—summer and winter. The hot summer lasts from May to October. The temperatures in the northern area of Egypt can reach more than 100 degrees. Because desert sands do not hold heat very well, nighttime temperatures can drop to freezing.

Winter begins in November and continues through April. During these months the climate is sunny and warm. In April, a powerful hot, dry wind called the *khamsin* usually blows across the desert. It kicks up dangerous sandstorms.

The Camel

Camels have existed in Egypt for more than 2,500 years. They are called the "ships of the desert" because they are used to carry people and heavy loads. Camels can walk easily on the shifting desert sand. They are also strong—a camel can carry about 600 pounds on its back for 30 miles. Because they can run up to 10 miles an hour, they are often used in races.

Camels are well suited to desert life. They have a third eyelid that allows them to see in sandstorms. They can close their nostrils between breaths to keep sand out of their noses.

Camels in Egypt are the dromedary kind. These camels have one hump on their backs where fat is stored. This fat keeps the camel alive when there is no food available. Camels can go without water for long periods of time. However, a camel does get thirsty—it can gulp 25 gallons of water without stopping.

What Makes Egypt Egyptian?

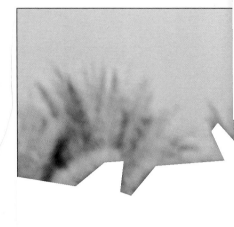

Egypt has the second largest population in Africa. Only Nigeria has more people. Most Egyptians live in small villages or cities along the Nile River. Together they make Egypt Egyptian.

Many different people live in Egypt. Long ago, Nubians moved into southern Egypt. They came originally from another African country, Sudan. The Copts live mainly in the center of Egypt. They can trace their roots back to the ancient Egyptians. Almost all Copts are Christians.

Berbers and Bedouin live in the Eastern Desert. At one time Berbers traveled in the desert with their herds of camels and goats. Now most Berbers work as farmers in villages. They usually grow wheat, fruits, vegetables, and olives.

Most Bedouin still live in small groups in the desert. They tend to their flocks of sheep, camels, and goats, and search for watering holes in the desert. Some Bedouin have settled down near towns and work as farmers.

Girls use a donkey to carry their crops.

The Mohammed Ali Mosque in Cairo

Arabs make up the largest group of Egyptians. Nine out of ten Egyptians are Arabs. Their ancestors came to Egypt about 1,400 years ago. In fact, Egypt's official name is the Arab Republic of Egypt. Arabic is Egypt's national language. Many people also speak English, French, and other languages.

Almost all Egyptians are Muslims. Muslims are followers of the Islamic religion. They believe in the Prophet Muhammad and study his teachings in a book called the Koran. Muslims pray five times a day. Whether in their homes, mosques, shopping centers, or parking lots, they will stop what they are doing to pray.

At home, most Egyptians wear the same kinds of clothes as do people in the United States. However, in public, they often wear traditional clothing. Some Muslim women wear a *niqab*, a long black dress with a veil over the head. Only the eyes can be seen. Other women wear the *hijab*, which consists of a dress that covers the body and a scarf that covers the hair. The face is uncovered. Men wear the *galabiyva*. This long robe fits loosely around the body. Some men also wear red-and-white checkered scarves wound around their heads to form turbans.

An Arab woman and child

The Egyptians have created some of the great wonders of the world. These ancient structures have lasted for thousands of years. They built fantastic pyramids in which they buried their kings and queens. The pyramids are located in the Egyptian desert. Mummies were buried in the pyramids with jewels, food, and furniture. The Great Sphinx is also located in the desert. This huge limestone statue, with the body of a lion and the face of a king, was built to honor an Egyptian ruler.

Egypt has contributed many things to society. Ancient Egyptians invented one of the earliest forms of writing called hieroglyphics. The hieroglyphic writing system uses pictures, called hieroglyphs, instead of letters. Hieroglyphs are found on the walls of ancient Egyptian tombs and temples. Egyptians also made a

The head of the Great Sphinx is six stories high.

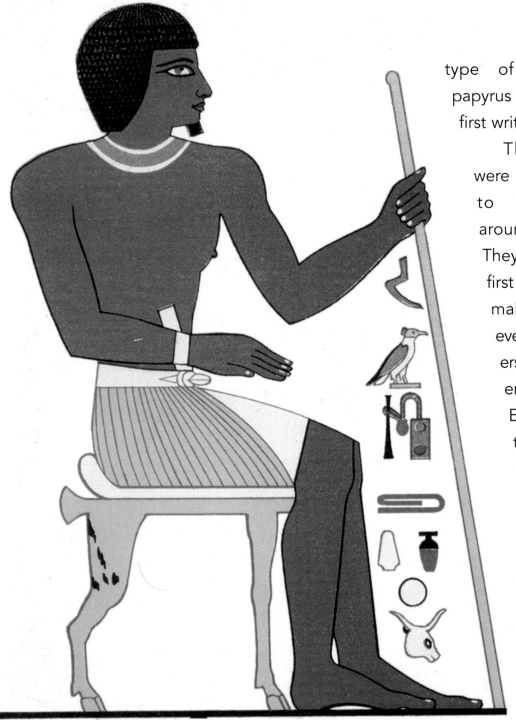

type of paper called papyrus and invented the first writing pens.

The Egyptians were the first people to wear makeup around their eyes. They were also the first to use yeast to make bread. They even invented checkers. Today, we still enjoy these early Egyptian inventions around the world.

Hieroglyphs found

inside a tomb

The Great Pyramid

The Great Pyramid at Giza was built about 4,500 years ago for King Cheops (Khufu). He was a wealthy ruler who was buried in the tomb.

The construction of the Great Pyramid was backbreaking and dangerous. Workers used ancient hand tools to cut 2,300,000 huge stone blocks of limestone and granite. Then they used ropes and special sleds to pull the blocks into place and fit them tightly together. Each heavy block weighed about two and a half tons, which is equal almost to the weight of twenty-five refrigerators.

The Great Pyramid stands more than 481 feet (147 meters) high—that is almost 50 stories tall! Its base is a perfect square. Each side of the square is more than 750 feet (229 meters) long. The Great Pyramid covers more than 13 acres (52,609 square meters). Almost ten football fields could fit inside it.

Living in Egypt

A little over half of all Egyptians live in small farming villages. These villages are usually close to the Nile River so that people can collect water for their crops and animals. Most village houses are made of mud bricks with straw roofs. The thick brick walls offer protection against the heat. The roofs help them stay cool too. When the nighttime temperature is high, many families sleep on these flat straw roofs.

Simple village houses have one to three rooms. These rooms are built around a courtyard where the animals are kept. Straw mats, benches, and a low table can usually be found inside.

Villagers are called *fellahin* (peasants). They usually grow two crops—one to feed their families and one to sell. A *fellahin* family often owns a pair of oxen, a donkey, and a water buffalo. These animals are used to

A boy leads his donkey to water.

A busy street in Cairo

plow fields and pull carts. The family may also raise chickens, rabbits, and pigeons. Pigeon is one of their favorite foods.

All members of a *fellahin* family work. The men plant and harvest the crops. The women carry water from the community well in large jars on their heads. They also cook and help grow the crops. The children take care of the animals and help their mothers carry water out to the fields.

Life in an Egyptian city is very different than life in a village. Almost half of the Egyptian people live in cities. Cities are filled with skyscrapers, outside markets, theaters, shops, and restaurants. They are also very crowded—in Cairo, about 100,000 people live in every square mile of space. Even though very few Egyptians own cars, traffic jams and sooty pollution are common problems in the cities. Most people ride

A felucca *sails across the Nile.*

streetcars, subways, buses, motorcycles, bicycles, and donkey carts.

City people may live in apartment buildings or in modern houses. But the poor live in slums. In many cities, nice houses exist right beside slums. Some poor people have even set up huts on the roofs of apartment buildings. They may also live in ancient tombs cut into hillsides outside of the cities.

There are many different jobs available in the cities. People can work for private businesses or for the government. Some work in offices, steel mills, or chemical factories. Factories that turn cotton into thread and cloth also employ many people. Others set up stalls in busy markets or narrow alleys to sell jewelry and other items. Since millions of tourists flock to Egypt every year, some people work in the tourist trade. They may drive a horse-drawn carriage called a *caleche*. Passengers ride in a *caleche* to see the sights. Or they may sail a boat called a *felucca*. Many tourists enjoy taking trips on these small boats with their white sails gliding up and down the Nile.

Although Egyptians like to eat in restaurants, most people also prepare food at home. *Ful*, a kind of flat bean, is used in many dishes. *Ful midammis* is the usual breakfast. *Ful* is simmered in a pot until the beans are soft. Then they are mashed with olive oil, lemon, and salt. Instead of knives and forks, most Egyptians use their right hands to eat. They usually eat their food with *aysh*, a round whole-wheat bread. They scoop up *ful midammis* with pieces of *aysh*. With their meals, Egyptians drink a sugary mint tea called *shy*. The afternoon meal is the largest of the day. It may include *lahma-misabika* (lamb stew) or *torshi*, a combination of pickled turnips and cayenne pepper. People also enjoy sandwiches of eggplant, tomatoes, beans, onions, and peppers wrapped in flat bread.

Late at night, when families gather for dinner, their meal may include kebabs, pieces of lamb or beef stuck on sticks and grilled over a fire.

Kebabs are a favorite Egyptian food.

Let's Eat!
Tahini ta'amiyya

Families serve this crispy treat throughout Egypt. It is a favorite food for children. *Ful* (fava beans) are often used in the recipe, but chickpeas are fine. Ask an adult to help you prepare it.

Ingredients:

1 can chickpeas
(garbanzo beans)

1 small onion, chopped

1/4 cup parsley, chopped

3 cloves garlic, crushed

1/2 teaspoon baking soda

1 teaspoon cumin

1 teaspoon coriander

1 tablespoon flour

1 tomato, chopped

1 bottle tahini sauce

1 package of pita bread

salt and pepper to taste

vegetable oil for frying

Wash your hands. Drain the chickpeas and keep 1 tablespoon of the liquid. Place the chickpeas, chickpeas liquid, parsley, garlic, baking soda, cumin, coriander, flour, and half the onion in a food processor. Blend ingredients until smooth. Pour into a bowl and chill in refrigerator for about forty minutes. Shape the mixture into twelve small balls. Fry the balls in hot oil until crisp. Remove from oil and drain the balls on paper towels. Sprinkle with salt and pepper to taste. Put three or four balls in a pita pocket with tomato, onion, and tahini sauce. Serves four.

School Days

All Egyptian children between the ages of six and fourteen are supposed to attend school. They can receive a free education at a public school. From ages six to eleven, children go to primary school. It is like elementary school in the United States. After five years of study, they take exams to find out what kind of secondary school they will attend. Those who do well on the exams will go to secondary schools that prepare them for an Egyptian university. Others will go to schools that train them to work in factories or in construction. Secondary school continues for six years.

Schools are open from late September through June with two weeks off for New Year's. Children attend school four days a week. School usually starts at 7:45 A.M. This is before the mid-day heat begins. Students assemble in the school yard to sing the national anthem. Afterwards, they enter their classroom and stand when

Girls listen closely to their teacher.

A classroom in a village school

the teacher arrives. Classes last about forty-five minutes. Students remain in the same room all day, with different teachers coming in to teach different subjects.

In the first two years, students learn reading, writing, and arithmetic. Starting in their third year, they begin to study science, social studies, music, and the Koran. In most public schools, students also learn three languages—Arabic, English, and French. Many classrooms have computers. In most schools, the day usually ends around 3:00 P.M. After school many children play basketball or soccer.

There are not enough schools in Egypt and they are very crowded, especially in the cities. Many schools operate on shifts. In these schools, as one group of students leaves at 11:00 A.M., another group arrives. Even then, there may be one hundred children in a classroom.

On Fridays, schools are closed. This day of the week is sacred to Muslims. The school day also changes during Islamic holy days. For instance, during the month of Ramadan, school does not start until 9:00 A.M.

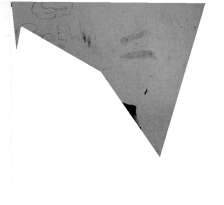

Students wear uniforms in a public school.

Homework

Schools are mainly run according to Islamic tradition. Following their beliefs, Muslim children must pray several times each day. Boys pray with male teachers in a group called a *salat el'gomah*. Girls pray separately. Prayers last from ten to twenty minutes each.

Students who attend public schools in cities must buy school uniforms. Boys wear pants with white shirts and ties. When the weather turns cool, they are allowed to wear matching jackets. Girls wear knee-length skirts and white blouses. Following Islamic law, many girls also wear skirts that touch the floor.

Almost all Egyptian children begin primary school, but by age fourteen about half drop out of secondary school. They take jobs on farms, in craft shops, or in factories to help out their families. Students who stay in secondary school and make good grades usually go on to a university. In a university, students study to become scientists, doctors, or teachers.

Egyptians take education very seriously. They urge their children to study and do well in school. They realize that the future of their country lies with their children.

School in Ancient Egypt

In ancient Egypt most children did not go to school. They were usually taught at home. Fathers taught their sons how to become farmers or how to work in a particular trade like pottery making. They only learned skills that would be useful in their future work. Mothers taught their daughters how to weave and cook. Girls usually stayed at home to help with household chores.

Only a few children went to school. They were the sons of the pharaoh or other important people in the kingdom. Their school was a room connected to the pharaoh's palace and temple. Priests and scribes taught students for a few hours each day. These boys learned to read and write so they could work as scribes. Scribes kept records and wrote messages for officials. Students learned to write a script called *hieratic*. Instead of learning how to spell, they learned to write symbols that represented words.

Just for Fun

Many Egyptian children surf the Internet, watch television, ride bikes, and play video games just like children in other parts of the world. They also spend time at the Cairo Zoo. It is one of the oldest in the world. It has a maze of beautiful paths and children can feed animals such as ostriches and giraffes. They can even hold the snakes in the reptile house.

A soccer game in the National Stadium in Cairo

The International Squash Tournament is held near the pyramids.

Egyptians like sports. The most popular ball game is soccer. It is played just about everywhere from the alleys of Cairo to the desert oases. Millions of people watch soccer matches on television. Cairo has the two most popular soccer teams—Ahly and Zamalek. They usually play at the Cairo Stadium.

Another favorite sport is squash. It is a very fast game similar to racquetball. Although teams sometimes play squash, usually one person plays against another. Players use long-handled rackets to hit a soft rubber ball off the walls of an enclosed rectangular court. The idea of the game is to bounce the ball off the wall so the other player cannot hit it. During August, the International Squash Tournament draws players from all over the world to compete on glass-enclosed courts next to the pyramids.

Middle-class and upper-class families often join sports clubs. These clubs are found throughout Egypt. Children can swim or play basketball, table tennis, volleyball, and tennis. They can also practice gymnastics, karate, and in-line skating. Most clubs have libraries and cafeterias.

During school vacations, many families travel. They enjoy going to the resorts on the Mediterranean Sea and Red Sea. They can stretch out on the sand, water ski, or swim. On these shores, the sands are gleaming white and the air is clean and warm. Children walk the boardwalks, hang out with friends, or even parasail over the sea.

The Sinai Peninsula is a good place to hike. Visitors enjoy the peninsula's rugged mountains, bubbling springs, and long-forgotten ruins. Bedouin guides show hikers the safest places to walk. Deep-sea diving and snorkeling in the Red Sea is another favorite activity. In the clear water, divers encounter beautiful coral reefs and schools of fish. People can go on "dive safaris" during which they may spend two weeks at sea.

Long-distance swimming is also popular in Egypt. About the middle of May, the Nile Swimming Race is held in the murky waters of the Nile.

There are many amusement parks in Egypt. Children can ride bumper cars or jump on trampolines at the Felfela in

A boy swims underwater in the Red Sea.

A Ferris wheel at a Cairo amusement park

Maadi. Dream Park, on the outskirts of Cairo, has rides and a go-cart track. Aquapark, also near Cairo, features waterchutes and a wave pool. A nearby theme park, Gero Land, has roller coasters and other thrill rides.

One of everyone's favorite spots is Dr. Ragab's Pharaonic Village on Jacob's Island, Giza. This is a theme park that looks like an ancient Egyptian village. People take a floating guided tour past scenes from life in ancient Egypt. They see temples, tombs, and statues of gods and goddesses. When they finish their tour, children can dress up like ancient Egyptians and have their pictures taken.

Game of Seven Bricks

Most Egyptian children play the same games as children in the United States. But there is one game that Egyptian children play that is not usually played elsewhere. It is called the Game of Seven Bricks. To play, seven bricks are first stacked in a pile. Players divide themselves into two teams. One team is the white team—for Upper Egypt—and the other team is the red team—for Lower Egypt. The object of the game is to knock down the pile of bricks with a ball about the size of a softball. Taking turns, each member of a team tries to knock down the pile. The team that succeeds in knocking down the bricks wins the game.

Let's Celebrate!

Egyptians celebrate several national holidays each year. On those days, just about everything closes—government buildings, banks, some businesses, and schools. These holidays include New Year's Day, May Day, and Armed Forces Day. Besides the national holidays, Muslims and Copts also observe several religious holidays.

Copts celebrate Christmas on January 7. Before the feast of Christmas, they refuse to eat animal meat and animal products for forty-three days. On the night of January 6, Copts attend a late-night mass, which is followed by dinner at midnight. On Christmas they exchange gifts. Afterwards they dress in their best clothes to visit with relatives and eat a large feast.

A *mulid* is a celebration in which both Copts

Girls laugh and play during a festival.

Swings set up on a Cairo street

and Muslims participate. During a *mulid*, people honor a local holy person or saint. Adults gather around a shrine and play special music and dance until they are in a trance. Children play on swings and enjoy other amusements such as puppet shows.

The Mulid El Nabawy is an Islamic holiday that celebrates the birthday of the Prophet Mohammed. Muslims sell special pink candies shaped like horses or dolls. They hang decorations from buildings and across streets. People wear their finest clothes and families feast together.

Ramadan, the holiest Muslim celebration, comes during the ninth month of the Islamic calendar. It marks

In the desert, a Bedouin man stops his work to pray.

During Ramadan, a family gathers to eat in a restaurant.

the month that an angel gave God's message to the Prophet Mohammed. The message was recorded as the first verses of the Koran, the Islamic holy book.

During Ramadan, Muslims fast. According to Islamic beliefs, they must not eat or drink anything from sunrise to sunset. Most businesses are closed during the day to allow people more time for prayer. People usually sleep late after spending many hours in their mosques.

Each evening families break the fast with large meals. They often serve a special treat, a sweet crepe deep-fried and then dipped in syrup. Restaurants also open up after sunset. They set up tents outside to meet the needs of their many customers. Under the tents everyone sits together at long tables to enjoy *sohour*, the last meal before sunrise.

Ramadan ends with a special festival called Eid al-Fitr. This festival usually lasts three days. Children have vacation from school. Some stores and restaurants also close for the celebration. Families gather and cook traditional foods such as *kahk*, cookies filled with nuts and covered with powdered sugar.

The Eid starts with prayers. Afterwards neighbors and families greet one another. Children receive

Dressed in new clothes, children celebrate the end of Ramadan.

gifts, usually new clothes to wear during the celebration. Many children also receive *eidyah*, a small gift of money from relatives. Children wear their new clothes and spend their *eidyah* at amusement parks, gardens, or public courtyards.

Whether gathering with family, greeting neighbors, wearing new clothes, or praying in a mosque, Egyptian festivals are ways of giving thanks and worship.

Fanoos

During Ramadan, children get time off from school. They also get to stay up late and play outside. Each child carries a *fanoos* (lantern). It is usually made of tin and colored glass with a candle inside. Some *fanoos* use batteries. The mosques and streets are full of colorful lights as children swing their lanterns back and forth singing, "Wahawi ya, wahawi iyyahah" (light of fire).

Egypt's flag has three horizontal bands. The black band stands for Egypt's history. The white band represents Egypt's government. The red band stands for the spirit of the Egyptian people. In the middle of the flag is a golden eagle. It represents the nation of Egypt.

Egyptian money is measured in units called pounds and piasters. Pounds come in banknotes, or bills, worth one, five, ten, twenty, fifty, and one hundred pounds. The banknotes are in Arabic on one side and English on the other side. Some banknotes show pictures of famous Egyptian landmarks such as ancient statues. Other banknotes show Islamic mosques. One pound equals one hundred piasters. Piasters come in banknotes worth five, ten, twenty, twenty-five, and fifty piasters. There are also twenty-five- and fifty-piaster coins, but coins are rarely used in Egypt.

Count in Arabic

English	Arabic	Say it like this:
one	wahid	WA-hid
two	itnan	it-NANE
three	talaatha	tha-LA-tah
four	arbaah	ar-ba-AH
five	khamsa	KHAM-sah
six	sittah	SIT-tah
seven	sgbah	SAH-bah
eight	tamanya	tha-MAN-yah
nine	tissah	TIS-sah
ten	ashara	AH-sha-rah

Glossary

artifact   Something made by humans, especially something made long ago.

dromedary   Type of camel with one hump.

ezayak (iz-ZAY-yak)   "How are you?" in Arabic.

irrigate   To bring water from a river or stream in order to grow crops.

mosque   Islamic house of worship.

mulid   Celebration in honor of a holy person or saint.

oasis   Place in the desert where underground water comes to the surface.

peninsula   Land surrounded on three sides by water.

republic   Form of government in which people vote for officials to represent them.

turban   A long cloth wrapped around the head to form a cap.

Proud to Be Egyptian

Anwar el-Sadat (1918–1981)

Anwar el-Sadat was born in a small village north of Cairo. He served as the president of Egypt from 1970 to 1981. In 1971 he changed the official name of Egypt to the Arab Republic of Egypt. He also invited foreign nations to trade with Egypt. Sadat led his country against Israel in the October War of 1973 to gain back lands that Israel had taken from Egypt. In 1978, Sadat signed a peace treaty with Israel's prime minister Menachem Begin. That year the two leaders shared the Nobel Peace Prize. But in 1981, Sadat was killed by a Muslim terrorist group.

Salma Shabana (1976–)

Salma Shabana is one of Egypt's best squash players. She was born in Cairo but raised in the country of Kuwait. Her parents were fine athletes who taught Salma how to play squash. When the family returned to Egypt, Salma played in the Egyptian Nationals, a major squash tournament. At age fourteen she won her first tournament. Salma went on to win the Egyptian Under 16 tournament three times. She also won the Under 19 Egyptian title seven times. In 1994 Salma won the All African

squash title. Although she had a knee injury in 1997, she continued to play against other top players. After getting married in 2000, Salma retired from the game.

King Tutankhamen
(ruled from approximately 1334–1325 b.c.)

King Tutankhamen is known as the "boy king." He was only nine years old when he became the ruler of Egypt. Most of the actual ruling of his kingdom was done by his adult advisor and by the general of the army. Not much is known about the king. He unexpectedly died at the age of seventeen or eighteen—he may have fallen from his chariot or he may have been murdered. He was buried in the Valley of the Kings at Thebes. In 1922, Howard Carter, an archaeologist, discovered King Tutankhamen's tomb, which had been hidden for more than 3,300 years. Most tombs had been broken into and robbed. However, King Tutankhamen's tomb was almost untouched. Inside, Carter found more than five thousand objects. The king had been buried within three coffins. One coffin was made of solid gold. A huge gold mask of the king's face covered the outer coffin. The tomb contained many objects that the ancient Egyptians believed the king would need in the afterlife—weapons, furniture, games, clothing, jewelry, and many golden treasures.

Find Out More

Books

A Look at Egypt by Helen Frost. Capstone Press, Minnesota, 2002.

Egypt by Shirley W. Gray. Compass Point Books, Minnesota, 2001.

Egypt: The Land by Arlene Moscovitch. Crabtree, New York, 1999.

Look What Came From Egypt by Miles Harvey. Scholastic Library, New York, 1999.

The Nile River: The Longest River by Aileen Weintraub. Rosen Publishing Group, New York, 2000.

Web sites

The *Enchantment of Ancient Egypt* at **http://library.thinkquest.org/CR0215618/** offers information on religion, the Nile, pyramids, mummies, games, and more.

Visit the *Yahooligans!* Directory at **http://www.yahooligans.com/around_the_world/countries/egypt/** for links to Egyptian history, religion, culture, holidays, and photos.

Video

In National Geographic's *Egypt: Secrets of the Pharaohs* viewers follow scientists as they explore the ruins of the pyramids. The video presents an exciting way to learn about the ancient rulers of Egypt.

Index

Page numbers for illustrations are in **boldface.**

About the Author

Lewis K. Parker is a teacher, writer, and editor in Connecticut. He is the author of many articles, plays, and books for young readers. He enjoys traveling and writing about various countries.